DARKNESS STICKS TO EVERYTHING

TOM HENNEN

Darkness Sticks to Everything

Collected and New Poems

Copper Canyon Press
Port Townsend, Washington

Printed in the United States of America

Cover Art: Susan Bennerstrom, *Wheat Silos near St. John*

Copper Canyon Press is in residence at Fort Worden State Park in Port Townsend, Washington, under the auspices of Centrum. Centrum is a gathering place for artists and creative thinkers from around the world, students of all ages and backgrounds, and audiences seeking extraordinary cultural enrichment.

LIBRARY OF CONGRESS CATALOGING-IN-PUBLICATION DATA

Hennen, Tom, 1942–
[Poems. Selections]
Darkness sticks to everything: collected and new poems /
Tom Hennen; [introduction by] Jim Harrison.
pages cm
ISBN 978-1-55659-404-5
1. Title.
PS3558.E496385D37 2013
811'.54—dc23
2012045654

3 5 7 9 8 6 4 2

FIRST PRINTING

COPPER CANYON PRESS
Post Office Box 271
Port Townsend, Washington 98368
www.coppercanyonpress.org

To my grandchildren, Aidan, Anna, Sean, and Josephine,
and my son Matthew, my daughter Colleen,
and my son-in-law David

He scatters the snow like birds flying down,
and its descent is like locusts alighting.
The eye marvels at the beauty of its whiteness,
and the mind is amazed at its falling.

THE BOOK OF SIRACH, 43:17–18

ACKNOWLEDGMENTS

The poems in this book—and the poet who wrote them—enjoyed good company along the way.

Jim Harrison: Patient with me all these years, and great encouragement from someone who understands what it is to be a dislocated farm boy.

Robert Bly: Much help from the start, about 1963, and ever since.

Garrison Keillor: Instrumental, through the American Humor Institute, in presenting me with the Bachelor Farmer Lifetime Achievement in the Arts award. Also an honor to be included in the anthology *Good Poems*.

James Wright: Kind words about the first poem I kept. Took time to talk—just the two of us—one afternoon at the U in Morris, Minnesota.

Tom McGrath: A long afternoon visit—springtime—in a small bar in Morris. We talked about writing, poetry, poets, and how to survive being one.

Bill Holm: Always a friend. Opposites attract.

Copper Canyon Press: All those good people who make so many poetry books possible. Special thanks to Joseph Bednarik, who did the editing on this book, and Kelly Forsythe, for the publicity efforts.

Paul Gruchow: Paul gave a talk to wildlife writers at Sand Lake Refuge while I was working there. I did not hear the talk—I was working on a barbwire fence. The next day, however, I took Paul to find Clovis buffalo wallow, which is located on a Waterfowl Production Area (Fed.). Years later Paul agreed to give a public reading only if I was included; afterward, he presented me his honorarium and refused to take it back.

Jim Gremmels, John Rezmerski, Gregory W. Bitz, Louis Jenkins, Mark Vinz, Beverly Voldseth, Thomas R. Smith, Dag T. Straumsvag: Let's go find Clovis buffalo wallow.

My brother Gary, my son-in-law Dave, and my son Matt for their many helps.

And especially my daughter Colleen, for all the work she invested so cheerfully, taking time from her own jobs to put up with an often puzzled old man. All is well.

Contents

from THE HOLE IN THE LANDSCAPE IS REAL
(1976)

from LOOKING INTO THE WEATHER
(1983)

from SELECTED POEMS 1963–1983
(1983)

from LOVE FOR OTHER THINGS
(1993)

from CRAWLING OUT THE WINDOW
(1997)

NEW POEMS

A Note on Tom Hennen

by Jim Harrison

Back in the 50s, 60s, and 70s, particularly the fabled 60s, the Midwest was certainly less lively literarily than our dream coasts. As a young poet I was reading everything, as young poets do, plus working in the university library. The two periodicals that meant the most to me were *Botteghe Obscure*, a multilingual periodical out of Rome in which I had discovered René Char, and *The Fifties*, edited by Robert Bly in Madison, Minnesota, which began explosively and continued so until recent years. Though certainly not universally loved, Bly pumped an enormous amount of oxygen into the heart of the Midwest's literature. At least on a regional basis Bly was as seminal as Ezra Pound was in the 20s, and along with his domestic introductions he vigorously introduced so many Spanish poets, from Hernandez to Vallejo, whose nocturnal melancholy seemed appropriate to the northern Midwest setting. The Spanish language nearly overwhelmed twentieth-century poetry but was late in being fully introduced in the U.S. Recently I relived some of the period when I had dinner two evenings in a row with Lorca's nieces in Madrid, which was unnerving. To get away from the Civil War so much of the movement was toward Paris but in the case of Lorca's brother and daughters it was New York and Columbia University. In more than thirty trips to Paris over the years I have loved navigating writers through the many immense cemeteries. I have visited Vallejo's grave many times quite near my favorite café, The Select, on Montparnasse, a wonderful location to read Vallejo and think of him tromping the neighborhood and turning in empty wine bottles he found for food money. This certainly wasn't the time for the comparatively lavish grants and readings nowadays. Not oddly from his roots, throughout Tom Hennen's work you sense the details of his humble origins which inform his work with a specific purity. I know of no poet in the United States better informed on simple rural life.

A curious thing has happened in the demographics of America in my own lifetime. Since the late 30s the U.S. has gone from a 75 percent rural population to a current 25 percent rural and 75 percent urban. Hennen is a poet of the way we used to be. As with Ted Kooser, he is a genius of the common touch. I have followed the work of no other American poet with greater pleasure and fidelity. He sings a bel canto simplicity better than anyone else. I recall at age fourteen reading Keats saying "The poetry of earth is never dead." It's sixty years now and I can think of no other line that stuck with me so close.

It was the greatest of pleasures to read this manuscript closely and to be reminded again how deeply the earth inhabits us. The Minnesota I've visited dozens of times is very similar to the rural areas of northern Michigan I grew up in, a botanical feast with profligate amounts of fresh water, lakes and rivers, and wild creature life, where the earth herself became your daily companion, also the domestic livestock for the small, fairly impoverished family farm, and the things of the earth stay with you forever, including the calf that liked to take walks with you and your dog, the birds you never stopped counting, the wildflowers you picked for mother's kitchen table.

Tom Hennen has had some hard luck. A physical injury in his outdoor work a few years ago left him unable to make a livelihood other than to house-sit his grandchildren, which seems like a fine job to me.

In a peculiar way I identify the geniuses of Ted Kooser and Tom Hennen with each other. This is not a huge step. They are amazingly modest men who early accepted poetry as a calling in ancient terms and never let up despite being ignored early on. They return to the readers a thousand fold for their attentions. Though I don't teach I often get sought for advice from young poets. I say I don't have time for you unless you're going to give your life to it. That's what it takes.

DARKNESS STICKS TO EVERYTHING

Did I Say This Before?

Once in autumn
I saw poplar leaves
Blast straight out from the treetop
And flutter through cold sunshine.
They even made a sound,
Some chatter they had learned from the birds.

Meanwhile, a lone monarch butterfly
Flew stiffly around and
Landed on a dry corn tassel
Where it hung with tiny feet
As the cornstalk shivered in the wind.
Left behind by its nomad tribe
What errand was it on?
Who had sent him
Wings thin as gold foil
To be placed carefully on a page
Of the illuminated manuscript of earth?

from **THE HERON WITH NO
BUSINESS SENSE**

(1974)

Home Place

The old house went down the basement stairs
And didn't come back up.

The people
The cows
The sheep
The pigs and the chickens
Have disappeared through a great hole
In the landscape.

Minneapolis

Blackened trees
Limbless from industrial accidents
Huddle on the outskirts of the city.

The swamp has become a supermarket overnight.
A heron with no business sense
Vanishes.

The hungry man from the woods
Feeds on loose change
Like a parking meter.

At night
The smokestacks sink into the ground.
Underground the soot changes hands.
The night shift moves slowly
Emitting a dim light from their mole eyes.

An odor of small lakes
Survives in the clothing of insects.

Wife

My wife, you believe me
When I say I am a white stone
As silent as the moon.
You follow me,
The cold air cracking your lips
As you pardon me
For the winter.
You are with me when my courage
Is as moveable as furniture.
In a dark room
Or the woods
You calm me.
You are the wild grass I lament
In late spring.

Thunderstorm Coming

Outside the granary door
The spilled oats growing
By leaps
Banging against the feed pails I'm carrying.

Under the yardlight
I see
It's really
Frogs and crickets
Passing each other in midair
Excitedly,
Almost shining.
As though they are the shape
Stars take
Close to earth.

Opening Day

First day of fishing season
The woods are crawling
With neurotic men.

Away from shore
At four dollars an hour
Boats are rocking
Empty.
Each shadow in the lake
A fisherman
Paralyzed,
Sinking
With tail and fins
And eyelids he cannot close.

Winter Twilight

It's winter now, and almost night,
The grass of the earth is dead.
My window sill has been put on crooked
So that I am chilled by air
Dark and cold.
Outside I can see no one,
And the last of the sunlight is being hunted down
By something frozen.

Lake Minnewaska Is Turning to Slush

Tracks lead to shore
Past an old boat punched full of holes
Toward a cabin
With kitchen lights already on.

Everyone has gone inside.
A gill net hangs from the garage wall
Dripping
Monotonous as an all-night rain.

Scaling the just-caught fish
Darkness sticks to everything.

Yard Work

Raking.
A garter snake
Underfoot.
Going berserk, I pound it dead.

The rest of the day
I jump
At each leaf.
Fear uncoiling
And winding into the deep brown grass.

Moving Day Again

Moving van
Left at dawn in rain.
About now
The kitchen table and chairs are
Gathering for breakfast
At seventy miles an hour.

We follow
A faint trail of rubber
Almost washed out.
Later
When we set up housekeeping
In a strange place
Holding hands,
The kids mumbling dreams,
You will have a hard time sleeping
Carried through the wet night
On a raft of small voices.

Old Women

Around highly polished bones
Clothing swirls
And floats.
Heavy mist
Woven from the dark backs
Of their children.

Old women bend their heads
To earth
While they zigzag
An inch or so
Above their grief.

Old Folks Home

On shadowy back porches
Rocking chairs
Are still
As fallen trees.

The old
Are imprisoned
In those bomb shelters
I see on the edge
Of country towns.

Strapped down
For a long voyage
They can't tell us anything
But only orbit
Far out in the gloom
Forever.

Going into the Woods

I see your breath
In midair—
a cloud
Hiding mosquitoes
Still lakes
Hot nights
You and me.
Wife, when you breathe the world fills up.

Let's go into the woods.
I'll listen
To your lungs take in red leaves.
Snow
Goose bumps
And the call of the freight train
Migrating south.

Let's lie here for a while
So still
That everyone will take us for rocks.

The New Arm

We all have
A new arm
Growing outward
From the shoulder
Filled with bullets.
It is leading us
Into continents
Where the people
Are disguised as colored maps.

We will sink
Arm first
To the bottom of liquid countries.

Many years from now
Some of us
Will surface in Asia
As white roots
Between cows' teeth,
And some of us
Will appear near our homes
With heavy arms we can't lift,
Making noises
On the wooden siding.

Getting Off the Bus

Getting off the bus on the plains
buffalo chips spelling out
GREYHOUND
while I dream of being a stalk of oats
fed to a mare.

Getting off the bus in the mountains
pine trees bent over
with tourists
who woke up to find their bodies covered with hair
after one night
alone.

Getting off the bus in the desert
where all the animals
hunch around,
well diggers
keeping secret the location of water.

Getting off the bus near the ocean
the passengers are left behind as buoys
the coastline advancing up my back
forming salt.

Getting off the bus
just as the duck
drops out of the V
in late autumn
with some unfinished business
up north.

Out of Work More Than a Year Still No One Answers My Letters of Application

In late winter
Afternoon sunlight
Doesn't budge the snowbanks
That have fallen whole into the backyard.

A forecast for more cold.
On the edge of the roof
Icicles are in deep conversation.
I pretend I belong and start talking.

Job Hunting

I want a job as a low cloud
Heavy as my wet wool cap
So if I'm hit
By lightning on the hill
I won't have to explain being out so late
Or how my socks got damp.

In the early morning I'll hang
Over evergreen branches
My ear lappers down
As lights go on
In the bedrooms
Alarm clocks ringing words
Of the first awake.

Almost frozen
I drift sideways
Across the sky
Rain turning to snow.

Looking at the Windmill

My kids come back from the long walk
With their hands full of stones.
They sense that my foundations
Are shaky.

They stay up late
To play with me
And humor me
While all night not talking
I duck in and out of air caves.

I am the distant windmill they know to look at
Moved by the least breeze.

Dirt Road

A feather plucked out and tossed away
By an old bird.
Shells of bugs
Whose names I don't know
Crunch
No matter where I put my feet.

After walking hard all summer
A goose voice
Tells me
I've caught up with autumn.

Woods Night

Primitive man
Tied to a stake
No leg
Breaking free
He is surrounded
Axe blows
Pine trees

He drifts
Overturned, past island
After island
Past midnight
Near my shore
I am still awake
Listening
Toward the lake

The last thing
I want to hear before going to sleep
Is that man
Splashing ashore.

Smelling a Stone in the Middle of Winter

I can't remember
What gravel and weeds are for.
This stone becomes important
And starts to act big.
I expect it to orbit the kitchen stove
Any minute now.
Near my nose
It gets
Bigger and bigger
Until it's a mountain
I'm lost on.

This stone is different
From the stone that grinds me down
All day
At work.

This stone smells as though
It's been wrapped in flowers
As your dress does
On a spring afternoon.
It's the hard feeling in my stomach
When I'm talking nonsense to you.

This stone is so inviting
Everyone wants to walk right into it
And become a fossil.

from THE HOLE IN THE LANDSCAPE
IS REAL

(1976)

A Winter Dawn on a Train

Faces come out of the dark
Pick a person
And settle down.

The steel tracks
Make understandable noises.
Their words are sparks
Flying off into the still dark fields.
Listen.
They explain
How to go for miles between towns
Without warming up.

Summer Night Air

Night doesn't fall
It rises
Out of low spots
Tree trunks
And the back
Of the old cow
I'm bringing home to milk.

Cold in the Trees

The hoot
Of the owl
Is large enough
To carry off a whole sheep.

Farm on a Winter Morning

All I can see are
Cows
And five A M
Milking machines
Hanging
On big teats.
The woman who hanged herself
Before breakfast
With a halter.
The price of oats dropping
On the way
To the house.
Me
And my father
Trying to break the ice
Between us.

Night near the Lake

Rain began quietly with the dark.
Cold water
Soaks the fur of wild things.
A smell of wet lumber is everywhere.
The night sways slightly
Tied to the dock.

Noises during the Night

A tree
Roars through town
Without stopping.
Animal dreams
Hum like batteries
In the frozen grass.
When the mind begins to snap
You can't tell it
From the sound of wind
Rattling empty milkweed pods.

Sunlight after the Pig Yard Flood

Washed up
On the mud
The old sow blinks.
Close to her belly little ones
Make the snorting noises of happy survivors.

In Falling Snow at a Farm Auction

Straight pine chair
Comfortable
In anyone's company
Older than Grandmother
It enters the present
With arms wide open
Wanting to hold another wife.

Knowing Nothing

The hole in the landscape is real.
I can walk through it and back again.
Every time I do
My clothes look baggier.
My hair sticks out.
My boots become untied.
My coat unbuttoned.
My education gone.
I don't care anymore how the world thinks.

I only know that the snow
Has reached my knees.

A Note to My State-Appointed Job Counselor

I'm a lousy escapist.
Troubles of the world roll off my back.
I lose my hearing
During job interviews.
I walk around in a daze
And pretend to know something.
The only talent I have
Is to be able to smell each new season
Before it comes
In the hair of women.

from LOOKING INTO THE WEATHER

(1983)

Before a Rain in Spring

The willow
Has a black trunk
Sticking up into the lifeless branches.
Thin as clouds
The branches
Swirl above the tree
They float off the ground
Like
The thousand frail thoughts
Of someone about to awake.

Tree Planting in Rain

Tiny spruce line up in a row
Behind me.
Their long toes grip the earth.
Together we disappear
Over the horizon.

After a Long Trip

The river is going to the Gulf of Mexico.
The moon on top the water
Doesn't move.
It's not interested in a
Trip to New Orleans.
Its light is already tired from traveling
250,000 miles
To shine on some trees.

Umbra

I've come from New Mexico.
One thousand years ago
I was an Indian poet
With two wives.
Now I'm white and short
And try all day to feel the earth
Through my work boots.

Part of My Job Is to Water Trees during the Drought

The spruce tree is dying.
I turn the hose on it anyway
The sun is under my shirt
Cooking my ideals.
Dirt in my nose and ears.
If the water truck hits me
I won't have time to repent.
My life and soul
Are tied up
Miles away from anyone
Who would think of putting their arms
Around me.

Independent Existence

A small pond comes out of the hillside.
On its surface
Hangs a frog imitating moss.
A willow leaf
Drops on the water
And is immediately still.
Autumn air penetrates the ground.
Wind hums endlessly
To the tangled grass.
When things happen here
There is no urge to put them on TV.

The Rain Puts Out the Burning Autumn Grass

Quietly as smoke
The bare plum trees
Cover the hill.

If You Bite a Wood Tick in Two with Your Teeth It Can Give You Rocky Mountain Spotted Fever

On cloudy autumn days
I miss
The weight on my skin
Of sunshine
And wood ticks
Thinking that what I hear at night
Is the noise of geese
Could be
Dogs barking
People hollering
Or the dirt road
Finally making a sound.

Usually an Old Female Is the Leader

Autumn has a mother.
Today
She's cold and wet.

A woman can draw heat
From a piece of furniture
Or a cloud.

A man
Can't get warm.
He tries to shoot down
The old hen duck
As she leads her flock away from snow.
His shotgun pulls him into the sky.

Autumn Waiting

Cold wind.
The day is waiting for winter
Without a sound.
Everything is waiting—
Broken-down cars in the dead weeds.
The weeds themselves.
Trees.
Even sunlight
Is in no hurry and stays
For a long time
On each cornstalk.
Blackbirds sit in bunches.
From a distance
They are quiet as piles of dark grain
Spilled on the road.

I Think of Bread and Water
and the Roots of a Tree All Wet

A description of the freeway
Lost
Looking for a city.
I come back
To geese.
Rain falls
On the parking meters
Glass and steel are shining
But people
Are dark
All the way through.

In the Shallows of the River

After one o'clock in the afternoon
Ice still
An eighth of an inch thick.
Night never disappears.
A glimpse of fur
Under the dark brush on the bank.
The aspens unmoving.
The goldenrod too
Is stripped down to its bare stalk.
In the cold
Even my thoughts
Have lost their foliage
And appear alone
Dry and narrow
In the flat air.

At Night I Dissolve

Fingers of mist
Arms and heart
Of fog
My voice
Crosses the threshold
A small cloud
Ascending
Toward the moon.

from SELECTED POEMS 1963–1983

(1983)

Light No Longer Seems a Gift

A field at night.
Yardlights and townlights reach me.
It's dark only
From my knees down.
As if wading.
The spruce
Pulls everything possible
Toward it
But lit up towns and farms
Don't move.

Where the land is flat
Light from the window
Travels in a straight line
Until morning.

In the Snowy Forest

As I dig a grave
For the old bitch dog
The ground steams
With each breath.
Here the earth
Is sandy
Loose even in winter.
We all have many bodies
Easily buried.
Behind us
The years rub together
And sigh
In the pine tops.
Only the snow that falls
Doesn't know
The heaviness of bones.

Graveyard

I can see right through these pine trees
Today in the rain.
They have gathered near the abandoned cemetery
On a prairie hill.
Because it's gloomy
They moan in one voice
Stand drooping in the mud.
Nothing can cheer them up.
Each one
Feels now
What it is to be uprooted
Taken far from home
And planted in a rainy graveyard.
Each one goes into the coming night
As if entering a forest.
Each one points silently at the sky
Its sharp needles
The color
Of eternal life.

Landscape of Night

Each night
Is a lake
That rises at sundown
Spreads itself thin
Laps at
The house lights
Fills up low shoes
Would make fish of us all.

Night Crawls On

Locked leaf by leaf
Into the shadows
The fragrance
Of plums
Moves
Sure as a road
Along the bottom of the night.

Animal of the Earth

For the first time I understand
I'm an animal too.
Bones.
Warm breath.
Moving shaggy arms
To encircle another.
Looked at
By beasts
That fly
Walk with four feet down
Crawl
On tiny scales that shine with flecks of spring.
I'm
The only animal
That wants to write a book
That moves so uncertainly through the cold
That spends so much time
Gazing at the sky
And listening for itself
Among the rustling sounds.

from **LOVE FOR OTHER THINGS**

(1993)

Early in the Season

I sit in the doorway of the granary
Chunks of moldy grain
Thin ice on the pasture slough
Winter still coming out of the boards
Cold on my neck.
The hours go past
One here
One there
Confused.
A flock without a leader.
Solitude has fallen
On the landscape.
Nothing makes a sound.
Even the lukewarm wind is silent
As it feels around
For grass.

Leaves in Autumn

It's impossible
To see the reflection of the crow
In the wet, dead
Leaf
But in the early morning dark
When people are trying
To learn to speak
To each other again
The leaf
Recalls a tongue and a voice
And a time when everyone could fly.

Finding Horse Skulls
on a Day That Smelled of Flowers

At the place where I found the two white skulls
Sunlight came through the aspen branches.
Under one skull were
Large beetles with hard bodies.
The other one
I didn't move.
Around them new grass grew
Making the scent of the earth visible.
Where the sun touched shining bone
It was warm
As though the horses were dreaming
In the spring afternoon
With night
Still miles away.

Picking a World

One world
Includes airplanes and power plants,
All the machinery that surrounds us,
The metallic odor that has entered words.

The other world waits
In the cold rain
That soaks the hours one by one
All through the night
When the woods come so close
You can hear them breathing like wet dogs.

Sweet Milk in the Wet Snow

Milk cow in the smoky snow.
Eyes dark as the water
In the box elder grove behind her.
Large flakes of snow pile up on the bones
That show through her back
As she eats at the snowbound hay in the trough.
Only the black spots on her hide can be seen.
She chews
And chews
Until her ruminations have taken her
Far from the cow yard.
Soon in the storm she will disappear completely,
Her heavy body adrift among the snowflakes.

Spring Follows Winter Once More

Lying here in the tall grass
Where it's so soft
Is this what it is to go home?
Into the earth
Of worms and black smells
With a larch tree gathering sunlight
In the spring afternoon

And the gates of Paradise open just enough
To let out
A flock of geese.

Country Latin

Some of the leaves had fallen
On the pasture pond.
The cows drifted
Black and white bodies, heads down,
Solemnly they grazed on drying grass.
Horns sparked in the sinking light.
A lone goose call drifted down
Lightly as a feather falling.
I jumped the fence
To fetch the cows for evening milking.
On the hill above the still pond I sang,
Ka Bas, *Ka Bas*.
The only Latin my father taught me
As I learned the dreamy habits of animals.
They came, as always, past the pond
As if truly happy to hear my voice.
The bristly hair on their backs
Lit golden by the sun
Just when dark mist began to rise
Around their cold hooves.

From a Country Overlooked

There are no creatures you cannot love.
A frog calling at God
From the moon-filled ditch
As you stand on the country road in the June night.
The sound is enough to make the stars weep
With happiness.
In the morning the landscape green
Is lifted off the ground by the scent of grass.
The day is carried across its hours
Without any effort by the shining insects
That are living their secret lives.
The space between the prairie horizons
Makes us ache with its beauty.
Cottonwood leaves click in an ancient tongue
To the farthest cold dark in the universe.
The cottonwood also talks to you
Of breeze and speckled sunlight.
You are at home in these
great empty places
along with red-wing blackbirds and sloughs.
You are comfortable in this spot
so full of grace and being
that it sparkles like jewels
spilled on water.

Clouds Rise like Fish

During July on the prairie
The pine tree stands alone on the main street
Of a disintegrating country town.
Its needles pump all day,
Still it cannot turn all the passing carbon monoxide
Into anything useful.
On its trunk ants are stuck in the resin.
From its top we can see the dark clouds
In the blue sky.
The island in the lake drifts even farther from shore.
Heat increases.
The afternoon begins its insect hum.
We can tell a storm is coming
By looking into each other's eyes.

Landscape in Pictures

There is the empty place
Between two evergreens
Where I meant to hang the hammock.
It frames the landscape.
Through it you can see
The hills and the valley
And the creek with no name.
One night I saw
A cottonwood throwing itself
At a sky full of lightning.
In the morning
Leaves were everywhere.

As I Write This Letter

I cannot wait for you any longer.
The warm breezes are gone.
The ripples in the water are frozen.
The forest is falling behind the rest of the landscape.
Snowflakes are messages sent
Into the cold night to keep you company
Until I arrive.
The earth is a letter circling the post office.
I am a foreign word scrawled on its surface.

Love for Other Things

It's easy to love a deer
But try to care about bugs and scrawny trees
Love the puddle of lukewarm water
From last week's rain.
Leave the mountains alone for now.
Also the clear lakes surrounded by pines.
People are lined up to admire them.
Get close to the things that slide away in the dark.
Be grateful even for the boredom
That sometimes seems to involve the whole world.
Think of the frost
That will crack our bones eventually.

from CRAWLING OUT THE WINDOW

(1997)

Crawling Out the Window

When water starts to run, winds come to the sky carrying parts of Canada, and the house is filled with the scent of dead grass thawing. When spring comes on the Continental Divide, the snowbanks are broken in two and half fall south and half fall north. It's the Gulf of Mexico or Hudson Bay, one or the other for the snow, the dirt, the grass, the animals, and me. The Minnesota prairie has never heard of free will. It asks you, quietly at first, to accept and even love your fate. You find out that if you fall south, life will be easy as warm rain. You wake up with an outgoing personality and a knack for business. The river carries you. You float easily and are a good swimmer. But if you fall north while daydreaming, you never quite get your footing back again. You will spend most of your time looking toward yourself and see nothing but holes. There will be gaps in your memory and you won't be able to earn a living. You always point north like a compass. You always have to travel on foot against the wind. You always think things might get better. You watch the geese and are sure you can fly.

The One and Only Day

There has only ever been one day and it happens over and over. No one knows where it came from. It slides through time, the prow of a ship through sleeping water. It bumps against the shore of daylight each morning and sets sail alone in the dark at night. Sometimes under the awful glitter of stars. Sometimes into a thickly falling rain that sends the animals back to their dens and causes the woods to drip and become the color of owls.

A Change of Weather

First sunlight ripples on the grass and still water. Then the air is filled with flying seeds. Long mosquitoes rise out of the hackles of the earth. The day brushes my cheek with a touch of cold fingers. Clouds leap in bunches from beneath the horizon and cover the ground as completely as a dark thought. Rain begins first deep inside where I can smell the dust I'm made of.

Grassland

Far south of the north woods, the red pine stands alone, sur-
rounded by hundreds of miles of space, able to see a county
away; it has been here for many years, its branches bent east
by the wind. New grass grows in thin clumps close to its scaly
trunk. Its long needles are green with spring. The landscape
all around is bare hills and wind. Only close to the pine tree's
bark is there the slight scent of forest, remote as a picture on a
postcard. From the tree a sound of longing as the wind blows
harder, and I know then that I've heard the sound of pining
in its original voice, the song within of those too much alone,
when they are the only object on the horizon, sky on all sides,
the day completely deserted, except for the sharp cold drops of
rain that have started to fall.

Autumn Mushrooms

Autumn mushrooms are growing under the fallen leaves and sprouting from the trunks of rotting aspen trees. Crisscrossing the forest floor are strange gnarled roots. One looks tough as a swollen fist, brown and hairy, punching up out of the ground from a fairy story about someone gathering firewood, just as I am doing, frost shaking down on my boots from high grass, piling on the leather toes, something from underground breaking through into the light, that will be talked about for years to come around a fireplace on sparkling cold nights when the winter is so long and the darkness so deep that the heart of the earth might break.

Shaking Off the Night

Just before dawn the fields are asleep, the grass is bent with dew. Spruce trees are the first to lift themselves toward the frail light, a flock of forest-colored birds rising. Wind the only traffic. In the house people wake up and come back to themselves in the way animals out all night return to their dens. No one knows where the other has been.

Waterfowl Hunting Season

Autumn has come again to the fading garden behind the farm-house. It has come with a wet day and thin, bare, shaking hard-wood trees. The hunted ducks and geese have been scattered into the cold sky by gunshots. It's as though they are the dark words earth has written to draw down the snow that makes us happy when we least expect it, coming from nowhere, bright flakes swaying tiny lanterns as they fall, leaving small drifts of light against the edges of the afternoon.

Night Storm by the Lake

From behind the hill full of heavy-leafed basswood the black clouds rise, thick as the humped backs of buffalo. Over the treetops they come, covering the evening light. Meanwhile, a slight breeze starts and lifts and falls in the long slough grass, quieting the mosquitoes. The lake cabin clutches the ground, its windows blinking. Over the hayfield there is a glow left by daylight. Even the stones seem to dig down deeper where they lie. Cattails on the lake's edge shudder in a sudden wind. The first thick raindrops fall, throwing dust into the air as waves of darkness slap the shore.

Sheep in the Rain

All day dark rain has fallen on the white backs of the sheep where they stand under the oak trees. Water drenches the branches and leaves. It penetrates the grass and ground. It makes the rocks shine. The wet hours drip from the edge of the barn, each one darker than the last as night comes. The sheep have the same glow as lit-up windows or small piles of new snow. If they were not there the darkness would be complete.

Crickets in the Dark

The farmhouse I'm staying in this year is a hundred years old, big, with six bedrooms upstairs and a walk-in attic. A farmer is letting me live here for nothing. He thinks my presence will discourage cattle rustlers. "Don't think they will bother if you're around. Don't worry." I don't. My shotgun is in the corner. I sleep in the living room by the open bay windows. A bouquet of cow manure and lilacs floats in from the nineteenth century. I am so far out on the prairie that there are no lights except mine, the stars', and the fireflies'. When my lights are off, only the stars and the fireflies are left to show the earth which way to turn, while in the darkness the crickets leap into the deep end of night, singing.

Prairie Heat Wave

Weather continues hot, baking the earth and its creatures. The sun breathes far away and we shudder, forgetting why, each of us a sun ourselves passing across the day, breathing too, our mood changing every few minutes, sparks flying from our hair-tips and striking the ground.

The day moves slowly as though under an anvil. The frightened smell of cut plants fills the afternoon as farmers chop alfalfa and sorghum. Trees cling to the earth as wood ticks to skin. The air is delirious with fear and heat and a stupor that lays things flat, letting the mind think only carnal thoughts.

Hand-planted pine trees are lined up in a row where I left them years ago, telling them not to move and they didn't, but now their young are growing, scattered around here and there with no order to their lives. Just as the younger generation everywhere, they are intoxicated by sunlight on their skin.

The Life of a Day

Like people or dogs, each day is unique and has its own personality quirks, which can easily be seen if you look closely. But there are so few days as compared to people, not to mention dogs, that it would be surprising if a day were not a hundred times more interesting than most people. Usually they just pass, mostly unnoticed, unless they are wildly nice, such as autumn ones full of red maple trees and hazy sunlight, or if they are grimly awful ones in a winter blizzard that kills the lost traveler and bunches of cattle. For some reason we want to see days pass, even though most of us claim we don't care to reach our last one for a long time. We examine each day before us with barely a glance and say, no, this isn't one I've been looking for, and wait in a bored sort of way for the next, when, we are convinced, our lives will start for real. Meanwhile, this day is going by perfectly well adjusted, as some days are, with the right amounts of sunlight and shade, and a light breeze perfumed from the mixture of fallen apples, corn stubble, dry oak leaves, and the faint odor of last night's meandering skunk.

Words in the Wild

Words are not common outdoors. Do you know how long it takes to find a word among the brush and tall bluestem? You can look all morning and the word you need will be miles away resting under a windmill, in the sun. When you do catch the word it is rare and alive and does not want to be put into a pen or tossed inside a poem made large as a house. It needs to be left with open places around it, trusted enough not to be staked down. And still it sometimes runs off in the night.

Spring Evening in Sparse Woods

I can hear the red-winged blackbirds calling, squawking as they do around a ripe cornfield, but it's still spring, the corn barely up. They make a noise now that rises with the cloud of new dusk. In the woods across the road the grass is trying to be quiet because night is coming, while the long branches of the lone evergreen are lifting up the half-moon as if it were a child.

Two Things

After the winter there is a day full of spring wind and on the plowing a small pond full of cold blue water so clear that looking into it I regain consciousness.

I wish it were different, but it is only when I am alone that the pine tree will let its needles surround me, shining, deep in its mental state of abnormal well-being.

By the Creek Bank

There is some secret that water holds that we need to know. I edge up close to the creek and peer into it for a revelation of some kind, an explanation of the world. Some things I think I know: that the sun rises, that the darkness heals, that animals are intelligent, that rocks are aware, that the earth has a sense of humor. The spring wind is blowing hard. The aspens along the bank make sounds of wood rubbing together, dry boards of an old house in a storm. Fair-weather clouds break loose on the bottom of the western horizon and drift one by one across the blue sky. Below me in the creek there is a clear pool full of minnows. I get down on my belly and carefully put my hand into the water among the small fishes. The minnows jerk past my numb fingers, swift as black seconds ticking. I cannot catch even one.

When Night Nears

Light leaves the earth a piece at a time, one hand letting go of
the tree branch while the other hangs on longer, slowly losing
its grip until it understands no help is coming and at last lets
go. It falls into the darkness taking with it people and dogs,
pine trees and butterflies, all the things we are so used to look-
ing at in the daylight. What is left is the dark that feels like a
body when you reach out, and the stars that glint so far off you
wonder what they are good for.

Two Crows and a January Thaw

In deepest winter two crows throw their voices into the blue air. Toward the end of the thawing day they rise on the still-mild wind, two notes of music that have escaped the songbook. They drift out of sight and back again. Their rough calls float down light as shadows growing long. Soon in the dark pine grove the crows and the night will be silent, empty, waiting to fill with stars.

Winter Nap

On a sunny winter afternoon I fill the stove with wood. When it is hot it makes the purring sound of the heart of a man revived after being dead for a few minutes. I pull a chair up to the heat, sit down with a book, and fall asleep. I leave my body and fly out over the snow-heavy fields. I sail about, avoiding treetops, ignoring airplanes, gliding past sheds full of the cold metallic silence of tractors. I've always had to work with machines, be a machine, or less, part of a machine. Only those who don't need to earn their living chained to technology can afford to be romantic about it. The machine breaks down the nerves. Its rhythm is different from the rhythm of life. Its steel and plastic voice wedges itself between each beat of the heart. It throws the whole body off center so that it can't digest moonlight or sunshine or understand a single chirping cricket. It makes it important to wake up from the winter nap to the smell of pine smoke, snow, and the light that comes in the frost-thick window, pale and lonesome as distant music.

A Man Too Much in Love

The first woman who left him pushed him over a cliff. At least that's what it felt like when he landed two months later. She had come to him out of the warm afternoon, dark red hair and innocent face. In the air was the perfume the ground has when it first opens up in spring, when all the birds become dizzy and some even drop dead with happiness.

The second woman who left him pulled all his teeth. At least that's what it felt like for two years and a day afterward. She had shining blond hair, a face that hit him suddenly as sun in the eye the first time he saw her. Only later was it like seeing a birch tree alone on a hillside, yellow as a lamp in the rain.

The next woman who leaves him will find that he will get up each morning anyway. That he will fall in love once more with window sills and grasshoppers, with long-legged pine woods, and words that can be used over and over again in the moonlight.

Things Are Light and Transparent

During the fall, objects come apart when you look at them. Farm buildings are mistaken for smoke among the trees. Stones and grass lift just enough off the ground so that you can see daylight under them. People you know become transparent and can no longer hide anything from you. The pond the color of the rainy sky comes up to both sides of the gravel road looking shiny as airplane wings. From it comes the surprised cry the heron makes each time it finds itself floating upward into a heaven of air, pulled by the attraction of an undiscovered planet.

Adrift in Winter

All anyone wants to know is when spring will get here. To hell
with dripping icicles, cold blue snow, silly birds too dumb to
go south, and sunlight gleaming off rock-hard snowflakes. I'm
sick of breathing air sharp as razor blades. I'm tired of feet as
hard to move as two buildings. I refuse to be seduced by the
pine tree blocking my path. Even though… just now, look how
it moves, its needles rubbing the sky-blue day. The glow it has
around its entire body. How perfectly it stands in the snow-
drift. The way both our shadows cross the noon hour at once,
like wings.

Out of Nothing

Snow began slowly. Only one flake fell all morning. It was talked about by everyone as they gathered for coffee. It brought back memories of other times. Dreams of ice skates, long shotguns waving at geese, cities lighting up somewhere off the horizon in the cold gray day. Only one snowflake, but it fell with the grace of a star out of the ragged air. It filled the day with a clarity seldom noticed. It stood out sharply as a telephone pole against the skyline of the winter we each keep to ourselves.

Report from the West

Snow is falling west of here. The mountains have more than a foot of it. I see the early morning sky dark as night. I won't listen to the weather report. I'll let the question of snow hang. Answers only dull the senses. Even answers that are right often make what they explain uninteresting. In nature the answers are always changing. Rain to snow, for instance. Nature can let the mysterious things alone—wet leaves plastered to tree trunks, the intricate design of fish guts. The way we don't fall off the earth at night when we look up at the North Star. The way we know this may not always be so. The way our dizziness makes us grab the long grass, hanging by our fingertips on the edge of infinity.

In the Sky of Winter

First day of winter and it seems all the insects are dead. None sail around any more or chirp or buzz or suddenly forget the art of flying above your soup. But they are there, under the leaves, burrowed into frozen plowing. Wings folded, legs tucked close. They are in the tiny cases of their bodies, alive, some of them, but still as fallen twigs or stones. Meanwhile, the sky, lonesome without its tiny aviators, has filled the air with snowflakes.

Looking for the Differences

I am struck by the otherness of things rather than their sameness. The way a tiny pile of snow perches in the crook of a branch in the tall pine, away by itself, high enough not to be noticed by people, out of reach of stray dogs. It leans against the scaly pine bark, busy at some existence that does not need me.

It is the differences of objects that I love, that lift me toward the rest of the universe, that amaze me. That each thing on earth has its own soul, its own life, that each tree, each clod is filled with the mud of its own star. I watch where I step and see that the fallen leaf, old broken grass, an icy stone are placed in exactly the right spot on the earth, carefully, royalty in their own country.

Autumn's Door

I have been following the seasons around and this one, autumn, is here again, new, turning the sumac red. The clouds are heavy, hang low, and scud across the horizon, dragging their dark, ragged edges over the brightly lit grain stubble. Sometimes it's as though a door has opened into the landscape so that we can see clearly each leaf, the sharp outline of each grass blade, and know for an instant just why we are here on this earth that is so loaded down with beauty it is about to tip over.

Early Spring in the Field

The crow's voice filtered through the walls of the farmhouse
makes sounds of a rusty car engine turning over. Clouds on a
north wind that whistles softly and cold. Spruce trees planted
in a line on the south side of the house weave and scrape at the
air. I've walked to a far field, to a fence line of rocks where I am
surprised to see soft mud this raw day. No new tracks in the
mud, only desiccated grass among the rocks, a bare grove of
trees in the distance, a blue sky thin as an eggshell with a crack
of dark geese running through it, their voices faint and almost
troubled as they disappear in a wedge that has opened at last
the cold heart of winter.

Heaven Has Two Sides

Frogs that sing in icy water on a sunny April morning know they are already in some kind of heaven. They tell us that the dimensions of one's body have nothing to do with the size of one's soul. Snakes are the other side of heaven, where praise is lazy and covered with sun-flecked scales on the warm edge of the rock pile, when we know that a fine spring day can curl and uncurl or disappear in the flick of a tongue.

Made Visible

The world is full of bodies. It's a happy thing and they should all be loved. Human bodies, raccoon bodies, blueberry and limestone bodies are the shapes we take when we want to be seen. How curious we are when we wake up and find ourselves in one of these new homes. The feel of snow, which we faintly remember, also the smell of wind, the sunshine's sweet taste. Sometimes I forget which body I'm in, like now, as I rest on my favorite log, an old aspen near Muddy Creek. The log, warm in the spring day, seems to lose more weight each year. It is dissolving as it dries. Before long it will be light enough to lift off the ground, rise past the treetops and into the sky, leaving behind the reminder that we are meant to spend our whole lives trembling in anticipation of the next instant.

Tracking the Breeze

Deer tracks are easiest to identify, sunk in the mud along a cattail slough or cutting sharp hearts in new-fallen snow. Even the myopic amateur is certain about deer tracks. It's the other marks that cause you to lose your confidence. The long-fingered imprint of the raccoon makes you think of a strange child barefoot, on all fours, wandering the creek banks. Or the claws of a porcupine that poke holes in the soft ground far ahead of its footpads. Tracking in dry dirt or over hard ground is an act of faith. It depends on how well you pick up scents. How much you have learned from the night air when the coyote is out giving lessons to the sheep on how to survive on the odor of starlight.

Gnats

The autumn smell of earthworms has attracted an off-course migrating woodcock who explodes like a feathery firecracker into the aspen thicket when I come too close. After all these nights of frost, most of the insects have given up for the year and have buried themselves in the duff. But here are tiny flies yet, small squadrons that dive and climb through the high reed grass. I don't know how these dark-eyed gnats have survived the cold beginning of fall. Perhaps autumn has a back door left open to a summer afternoon in the world next to ours.

The Ants, a Feeble People

Those fall days are best when the afternoons warm up enough to take the edge off, and my ragged work jacket is too heavy, but I leave it on anyway. In the old gravel pit I take a break from cutting wood. Aspen and cottonwood have grown up since the pit was abandoned. Some have become real trees and show their age with broken limbs and lightning scars. Under the shivering yellow leaves there is a large ant mound with only a few big ants on it. They have sealed it against the coming winter and now make one last check for open holes. I cannot see how they will be able to get back in. I wonder if they have sacrificed themselves for the others. They are calm. When they stop to rest, the sunlight seems to give them pleasure. I sit beside them for a long time while we feel sorry for the ones safely inside.

Sheep in the Winter Night

Inside the barn the sheep were standing, pushed close to one another. Some were dozing, some had eyes wide open listening in the dark. Some had no doubt heard of wolves. They looked weary with all the burdens they had to carry, like being thought of as stupid and cowardly, disliked by cowboys for the way they eat grass about an inch into the dirt, the silly look they have just after shearing, of being one of the symbols of the Christian religion. In the darkness of the barn their woolly backs were full of light gathered on summer pastures. Above them their white breath was suspended, while far off in the pine woods, night was deep in silence. The owl and rabbit were wondering, along with the trees, if the air would soon fill with snowflakes, but the power that moves through the world and makes our hair stand on end was keeping the answer to itself.

Soaking Up Sun

Today there is the kind of sunshine old men love, the kind of day when my grandfather would sit on the south side of the wooden corncrib where the sunlight warmed slowly all through the day like a woodstove. One after another dry leaves fell. No painful memories came. Everything was lit by a halo of light. The cornstalks glinted bright as pieces of glass. From the fields and grove came the rich smell of mushrooms, of things going back to earth. I sat with my grandfather then. Sheep came up to us as we sat there, their oily wool so warm to my fingers, a strange and magic snow. My grandfather whittled sweet smelling apple sticks just to get at the center. His thumb had a permanent groove in it where the back of the knife blade pressed. He let me listen to the wind, the wild geese, the soft dialect of sheep, while his own silence taught me every secret thing he knew.

Backpacking among the Thistles

A cold June morning. I am at work out in the country, wearing a metal backpack and spraying Canada thistles with the chemical 2, 4-D. Who can I tell who won't consider me a villain, a herbicidist, a ravager of the earth? The marsh is full of wildly singing birds. Soon the sun will warm things up. I move deep into the high thistles. Mosquitoes cover my face, fill my eyes and ears. The straps pull me down as I walk. I can hear, from a mile away, a rifle firing at short intervals.

After Falling into the Slough in Early Spring

Back in the water, my clothes wet again. The loafing log I'm putting out for the ducks to rest on floats patiently near me. I stand there for a long time, so the teal start to swim close, a marsh wren tries to land on me, and the cricket frogs start up their calls that sound like pebbles hitting together. I scoop up one of the tiny frogs floating by on an old leaf and hold him just tight enough. His dark eyes have no fear in them. His body is no more than an inch long and brown as tobacco. I know I'll never see him again once I let him go so I hold on a bit longer. If nature has a soul, this tiny frog could be the shape it takes. And if that soul makes a noise, it might sound like small stones being hit together.

Leaving and Return

How long the rain falls. It throws itself from the black sky wrapped around a tiny piece of dirt. The trees shake their leaves with a sound like wet glass breaking. Light from the window is smeared against the night. To the spring wind we are nothing but dust it could carry off if it wanted. It could lift us into the clouds where we would have to wait until we became the center of the raindrop, and then, some dark day, we would leap toward earth and the roof of a well-lit house.

What the Plants Say

Tree, give up your secret. How can you be so satisfied? Why don't you need to change location, look for a better job, find prettier scenery, or even want to get away from people?

Grass, you don't care where you turn up. You appear running loose in the oat field, out of a crack in a city street. You are the first word in the vocabulary of the earth. How is it that you are able to grow so near the lake without falling in? How can you be so alert for the early frost, bend in the slightest breeze, and yet be so hard to break that you are still there, quiet, green, among the ruins of others?

Weed, it is you with your bad reputation that I love the most. Teach me not to care what anyone has to say about me. Help me to be in the world for no purpose at all except for the joy of sunlight and rain. Keep me close to the edge, where everything wild begins.

Outside Work

On these autumn days when even the sunshine is cold, I feel happily lonesome as the wild bee that comes looking for one last flower before the snow. I move drowsily through the warm spots in the day. My muscles, too, are stiff if I drift into the shadows. The sudden chill makes me shudder. I move through the floating spider webs and reach a clearing in the sunlight where the earth itself is about to fall asleep into its own daydream. In the dream the bee and I are both children in the same family. We have never left home. Everything tastes like honey.

When Storms Come

When a great rainstorm comes out of the southwest, rolling dark over the grassland with crackling white thunderbolts that strike as close as your hair, then all the things made by humans become small, and all the things we have learned take up almost no room at all. Towns are perfectly still. Farm buildings disappear among the rain-shiny groves of trees. In the farmhouse we are quiet. In the barn doorway we don't move, thinking we won't be seen, while the earth rocks, and the lightning seeks to touch—like a tap on the shoulder—its next partner for the dance.

Walking through a Narrow Strip of Woods

Pines as always pried at the sky with their tips, ignoring the wind around their trunks. I dodged the stinging underbrush as it was snapped off. Sometimes a branch would hit my cheek. I thought for an instant how ungrateful nature is. I noticed how my boots crunched the new thin snow, pushing the flakes together. I remembered the last time I was in the city. How the grass grew in the sidewalk. How the spruce tree was still standing in the morning next to the parked car. How the singing coming from within the tree might not have been birds, that the thread nature uses to connect all things together is joy. When I think of this in a narrow woods I fill with shame for all the cruel things I've said about cities, for they too will dissolve as bones dissolve, as the rain is broken by the ground, and because we are allowed to pity everything except ourselves.

NEW POEMS

An Autumn Gift

Red maple leaves
Lie just so
In the tall faded grass.
Happy to do it.

Some Music

On the north side of the small lake a lone and age-battered cottonwood tree sings to itself. Early in the fall its leaves are smooth and yellow. When the wind blows through them they sing mostly of summer, with only a note or two of a rare cold night. When the leaves begin to fall the song changes every day. As more leaves fall the tone becomes uncertain, as though the composer is worried about something. But it only adds depth, and does not depress the birds. Often they join in with a simple piece of their own.

After the killing frost, leaves fall like unpredicted rain. Sometimes they float and sail far from the tree. Sometimes they come down straight and make piles of cool sunlight on the ground. Every day the leaves in the trees are fewer. The music keeps on, a smaller song that goes out over the lake and into the blue air above it.

Red-winged blackbirds migrating south come to help. They fill the empty places on the branches. They sing the same cheerful song they sing in spring. They may know no other. One day they scatter suddenly, dark leaves falling up, into the stormy clouds. The tree is again alone to sing its song, now with only a few broken dry leaves, low and scraping as a whisper.

Today the tree is silent. On the twigs, close to where the leaves once were, there are sharp-pointed winter buds. Inside each one a sheet of next year's music in the shape of a tiny green leaf, tightly curled, carefully waiting. Nearby, the lake is quiet as frozen stone. The dark gray sky that had taken all the songs up to itself now sends back thick white snow that falls with a sound too soft to hear.

Wild Aspen Leaves, October

Icy wind blows
Across the narrow river.
A household of pale trees in the small dusk
Of early afternoon.
If the sun were a tree
Its leaves would be this shining color
And they would drop
Over the toes of my boots
Ankle deep.
When I step
There would be the sound
Of light breaking.

Wet Autumn

Early morning, everything damp all through.
Cars go by. A ripping sound of tires through water.
For two days the air
Has smelled like salamanders.
The little lake on the edge of town hidden in fog,
Its cattails and island gone.
All through the gloom of the dark week
Bright leaves have been dropping
From black trees
Until heaps of color lie piled everywhere
In the falling rain.

Skift

In flakes, in the shape of pellets and pills.
Snow drifting, sailing, wind driven.
A hatch of crystal insects. One race or many?
Genus, species not classified or understood. Habitat air and
sky and earth. Lives in groups. Small and large. Starts out
alone but soon in crowds of snow, in piles, in banks, in drifts,
in heaps, in shovelsful.
A skift of snow.
Skift, a word my father used for a very small amount of snow,
but more than a trace, hard and fine as bread flour. It appears
only on the coldest winter days. It comes when you are not
looking: busy throwing hay down from the loft for the milk cows,
or lighting a cigarette with your back to the wind, etc. It's
the layer of dry snow that skids over the patches of bare ground
in below-zero wind when your eyes are freezing shut. Skift snow
spreads itself in thin ribbons on the clear ice of puddles
frozen to the dirt.
Skift snow frightens all the birds away except the chickadee
that has no room in its little body for an ounce of fear. The
only sound of skift snow is a whisper as it brushes across
the crusty winter afternoon. No matter. The chickadee will sing
the same short song it has been singing since
it left the ark, even as the next ice age slides in
on a skift of snow.

Found on the Earth

The simple words no longer work.
Neither do the grand ones.
Something about
The hanging bits of dark
Mixed with your hair.
The everlasting quietness
Attached to the deserted barn
Made me think I'd discovered you
But you already knew all about yourself
As we stood on the edge of a forest
With your dress as languid as the air,
The day made of spring wind and daffodils.
Then the sky appeared in blue patches
Among slow clouds,
Oak leaves came out on the trees,
Grass suddenly became green,
Filled with small animals that sing.
All the parts of spring were gathering.
The earth was being created all over again
One piece at a time
Just for you.

Credit to Keats, I Think

Here by the river drifting
Clouds on its surface flat and white
As upon reflection the sky
Doesn't know up from down
So fish might toss
Themselves onto the grass
Wet flashes spilled
To gnaw nibble bite
The edges of the summer morning
To cause bunches of light
Gathering on the brink of birch woods
To bristle brightly
As blinding fur.
The day has begun as a puzzle
Of surprise
With no answer
But only a leap
Of wild surmise.

Corn Picking 1956—Afternoon Break

I needed a heavy canvas jacket riding the cold red tractor, air an ice cube on bare skin. Blue sky over the aspen grove I drove through on the way back to the field, throttle wide open, the empty wagon I pulled hitting all the bumps on the dirt road. In the high branches of the aspens little explosions now and then sent leaves tumbling and spinning like coins tossed into the air. The two-row, tractor-mounted corn-picker was waiting at the end of the corn rows, the wagon behind it heaped so high with ears of corn their yellow could be seen a mile away. My father, who ran the picker, was already sitting on the ground, leaning back against the big rear wheel of the tractor. In that spot out of the wind we ate ham sandwiches and doughnuts, and drank hot coffee from a clear Mason jar wrapped in newspaper to keep it warm. The autumn day had spilled the color gold everywhere: aspen, cornstalks, ears of corn piled high, coffee mixed with fresh cream, the fur of my dog, Boots, who was sharing our food. And when my father and I spoke, joking with the happy dog, we did not know it then, but even the words that we carelessly dropped were left to shine forever on the bottom of the clear, cold afternoon.

Prairie Grain Elevator

A warm spring wind blew hard from the southwest. In the prairie town it whistled up the dusty road and sang itself around roof corners. If anyone had faced into it, grit would have pelted their eyes. Inside the elevator our old truck was being unloaded of wheat we had saved over the winter so we could sell it now for new seed to plant and spark plugs for the tractor. The elevator had a large alleyway with big doors open on both ends to drive into to unload where our truck was tipped up, dumping wheat onto the floor grates where it disappeared into the pit beneath, fast as water draining away. Down the alleyway grain dust mixed with street dirt flew in circles and burned in your eyes like tiny lit matches.

Being a kid, I stood out of it all, out of the grit, out of the dust, out of the dirt storm. In the late morning quiet tumbleweeds rolled north through empty streets. Wind blew sunshine against the last of the snowbanks causing clear puddles to appear, glinting with silver light. From the big doorway a man came out into the clean air, his face nearly covered in a red bandanna. When he saw me he pointed his finger quick as a six-gun and laughed when I dropped like a cowboy, then he was gone in a puff of dust.

In the Ripe Wheat Field

Leaving my hand suddenly empty,
With the reckless choice
Of ancient intelligence
The grasshopper jumps
Into his other body
The one with black wings
That carries him to the fence line
Where the goldenrod gathers
In the noonday sun,
Beyond my harm
Beyond my help
Before I can explain the meaning
Of the word *winter*.

Outside Hay Pile 1956

Dark summer nights lead into autumn
And the frost that floated about me.
Cold air from the shadows flowed over me
Onto the sheepskin coat I wore
That smelled of the barn and tractor oil.
On my back in the hay pile
I watched the Milky Way
Turning through the far-off dark
Like a country road,
Stars billowing thick as dust clouds
Behind a pickup truck.
If someone were to ask where the road leads,
Who would dare answer?
When the big dog pushed his head into my face
I held on to his fur with both hands
To keep from falling into the sky.

Inside a Raindrop

Low sky full of gray drizzle about a minute from ice. The dog, who is oblivious to discomfort, has noticed both the scent of the Rocky Mountains seven hundred miles to the west and wolves five miles northwest. I'm carrying a small-bore shotgun (.410 gauge), happily kicking through the tall late-fall grass along the farm creek waiting for a ring-neck pheasant to break from cover with a crackle of broken music so disturbing it would make a stone jump. Later, the rooster pheasant, shot dead, tied with twine around its legs to my waist, its feathers sparkling in the dull light. I stop to rest in a row of hand-planted spruce. Water hanging on every needle, and inside each drop the image of a boy, his .410, the hanging pheasant, the yellow dog, all in sharp focus, complete color, and upside-down. Still a mile from the warm farmhouse. Dark coming fast from the east. The wolves close. The boy unaware. The big dog ready.

Wolf's Light

Gloaming is the thick dusk that comes when the sun has set,
when the last of the daylight has been left stranded with
nowhere to go but down into the twilight where light and
dark and air float together close as fog to the ground,
with ripe corn and yellow aspen. It is the time made
especially for wolves, when the earth wades into the shallows
of the night. If then I was hunting along the creek
with my dog, I would lose my place in the landscape, something
dangerous had come near as the autumn grass that brushed my legs.
We smelled the sudden odors of cold moving water and dusty fur.
In silence the dog and I would turn toward home. All the way
back the padding of other feet, so lightly it could have been
breeze. Miles of blackness had us surrounded. By the barn the
electric light pole, its lone bulb dimly burning, one candle
against all the dark of outer space. Close by us still were the sounds
that had followed us, fallen leaves were quietly stirring. No
matter how often this happened, not once were we devoured.
Not once did we wonder what worse we were saved from.

The Weasel Becomes an Ermine

Shorttail weasel, the ermine of winter, I wondered if he was living in the walls of the farmhouse or just on a night visit for mice. It was near the end of fall. The bare plum thickets in the ravines hanging dark as smoke. Sunlight with a weightless touch on the buildings and corn stubble. Close to the creek the weasel would appear unexpectedly, because a weasel is always unexpected, except to chickens and mice. The weasel seemed to travel by being here, then there. It could be it ran, it did have feet. But I suspected other means. Though I do know they can walk slowly if you are looking for arrowheads on a brown hill in a cold wind. Then they will follow you with great unnerving interest, coming close enough to kick. I have noticed that they do not care that we use their names as an insult, that they remain curious about us, that their eyes are too shiny and black to look into without danger. At what moment they turn white, become an ermine, and are mere weasel no more, is a secret safe with me.

Under a Dark Sky

The sky has become too heavy for itself
And bumps the hilltops,
Catches on wooden fence posts.
Then the first snowflake
Is pushed out of its nest.
A fast learner, it drifts and turns
With precocial skill as it falls
Toward the fur of a rabbit silent under the brush.
A wet frozen sky dropped on the ground
Is too much to lift.
But one snowflake is weightless.
Like an empty thought
No two
Are exactly the same.

Winter, Thirty Below with Sundogs

The sun came up chased by dogs
Across a field of snow.
As they passed the pile of broken logs
Frost fluttered in the air
Between the birch trees
Standing in that spot exactly
Where the ridge becomes a hill.
In another thousand years
Sky and woods and land
Will have come to be there, still.
And still pursued all day, a winter fox
Too smart for dogs,
The sun goes in animal delight
Over the farthest edge of earth
Not far ahead of night
And jumps into the dark pool
With a last great splash of light.

Midwinter

This morning cricket frogs
And dry warm snakes come to mind
As the eaves of the house sag with ice,
While across the road
Small trees haul snow by the armload
Deeper into their patch of woods
For reasons they don't explain.

At First I Thought

The blue jay
Was the last leaf
To fall
When it rocked
From side to side
And slowly tumbled
To land on the snow
Weightless
As a piece of sky
Broken off
The cold blue place
Where winter keeps
The number zero.

Late March

A dark day raining.
A bright flash
Of blue jay disappearing
Into black folds
Of a dripping spruce tree.
Bark of ash and apple tree shine
In the dim drizzle.
The woodpecker's song this afternoon
Is a chipping noise,
A sound that puts little dents
In the wet air.

In the Late Season

At the soft place in the snowbank
Warmed to dripping by the sun
There is the smell of water.
On the western wind the hint of glacier.
A cottonwood tree warmed by the same sun
On the same day,
My back against its rough bark
Same west wind mild in my face.
A piece of spring
Pierced me with love for this empty place
Where a prairie creek runs
Under its cover of clear ice
And the sound it makes,
Mysterious as a heartbeat,
New as a lamb.

Plains Spadefoot Toad

Toads are smarter than frogs. Like all of us who are not good-looking they have to rely on their wits. A woman around the beginning of the last century who was in love with frogs wrote a wonderful book on frogs and toads. In it she says if you place a frog and a toad on a table they will both hop. The toad will stop just at the table's edge, but the frog with its smooth skin and pretty eyes will leap with all its beauty out into nothingness. I tried it out on my kitchen table and it is true. That may explain why toads live twice as long as frogs. Frogs are better at romance though. A pair of spring peepers were once observed whispering sweet nothings for thirty-four hours. Not by me. The toad and I have not moved.

Longing for a Small Rain Down to Rain

Since we parted
So much space
So much emptiness.
I've been trying to cross it
By imagining
Each oak tree, pine, and long road.
Between us the moon at twilight
Two stars
And the planet Venus shining
Bright as a newly thawed lake.

When the rain comes down,
When warm wind drives it over the prairie
Into the woods
To hit the dark window
The storm will rock the night
In wild affection
As water dances off the roof,
With the sound of horses
Running loose in the meadow.

Another Toad

The half-grown prairie toad will stay motionless in my fist with just its head poking out, eyes bulging (how can you tell?). I think it likes the warmth of my hand. Also, it may be composing itself to be eaten, a natural assumption when in another's grasp.

Sometimes when you open your hand the toad will not move for thirty seconds. Suspecting a trick? Not believing its luck? But soon it jumps recklessly as a frog into the empty air. It then sits quietly on the ground near the shallow pond of rainwater, its sides going in and out, a rock breathing, not blinking, letting the sun shine directly into its eyes.

What Can You Expect of Spring

The moon in daylight, slightly lost
Among the white chickens,
Sniffs the warm spring air
Scratches the flower scented dirt.
What sounds then
Do new leaves make unfolding
On the box elder branch
But the popping in our ears
When we come up for air.
Underfoot rumbling
As a church organ
When the music is done
The doors shut
While the newborn day trembles
Shiny yet
As if wet paint drying
In the sun.

After Reading John Clare on Thoughts of a Cow

There are deep hoofprints in the soft ground around the wooden water tank. A steel windmill with its fan blades spinning free in the summer wind. No water pumping because the connecting lever is not in gear and the tank is full. Thick green moss floats here and there on the water's surface. Blue sky and white clouds reflect in the pool, pulled out of heaven in a piece just the right size to fit the old round wooden tank. The cow yard is empty, the cows in the far pasture, strolling its hills for grass, slowly, with quiet pleasure as if on a boulevard in Paris, France. Nothing about a cow yard enters their thoughts until late afternoon when I come with the dog to fetch them home. Then they amble, dust stirred from its summer stupor by their hard hooves that kick up the smell of dirt and powdered dung. After the long walk from the pasture they remember they are thirsty. Now in a hurry, they crowd around the water tank. They drink and drink. When one raises her head, water and setting sunlight drip from nose and muzzle. With a tin cup I drink icy water from the pump and pour some into a pan for the dog. The cows are dry of milk until fall. Now all they need do is sleep. From the east dusk is sliding across the fields. Frogs and crickets are tuning up, fireflies cannot wait and are airborne before the sun is completely down. The summer night

settles weightless as a feather on the grass. The windmill turn-
ing, cold water running out of the iron pipe into the tank, far-
off bells, and the murmur of starlight falling on water.

June, with Loons

Heat heavy as an overcoat by midmorning,
The scent of pine thick as mud.
Two loons call loudly close to shore.
They sound deeply disturbed,
Which means everything is fine.
The sky a deep pretty blue,
That selfish young blue
That will not let even one small cloud
Anywhere near it.
Because of its beauty, we don't care.
The lake, as usual,
Has taken its mood from the sky,
Its color also,
The blue that breaks hearts.
Light falls out of the summer day
Onto the surface of the water,
Delicate and silent,
Perhaps as rain falls in a different world
Or at the other window,
The one we are not looking out of.

Minnows I

I put the bundle of small pine trees on the shady side of the truck so they wouldn't dry out. Below the hill a clear, fast creek ran between steep banks. Minnows in the pools turned in tight bunches, this way and that, flashing white bellies, then showing dark backs. They slipped through cold water that was only a few days past being snow. The water had a sweet tang, a taste of frost, and when it moved over the rocks it made a kind of music, as if it were an absentminded bird trying to remember the melody of spring.

Outdoor Photos

Find a quiet rain. Then a green spruce tree. You will notice that nearly every needle has been decorated with a tiny raindrop ornament. Look closely inside the drop and there you are. In color. Upside down. The raindrop has no instructions to flip us right-side up. People, dogs, muskrats, woods, and hill, whatever fits, heads down like quail from a hunter's belt. Raindrops have been collecting snapshots since objects and people were placed, to their surprise, here and there on earth.

Raindrops are fickle, of course, willing to substitute one image for another without a thought as we pass by them. Our spot taken by a flash of lightning or a wet duck. Still, even if we are only on display for a moment in a water drop as it clings to a pine needle, it is expected that we be on our best behavior, hair combed, jacket buttoned, no vulgar language. Smiling is not necessary, but a pleasant attitude is helpful, and would be, I think, appreciated.

What the Bees Found

Sunshine dries the dew. The prairie springs thick green. Soft in the ravines, low and lush in the new grain, tough and wild in the river bottom. Wind and sun move over it all in waves of fresh light. June is the month of ease on the prairie. Plants grow without pause. Every creek runs with fast water. All who live here were born rich.

One at a time the sheep are let to pasture like fair-weather clouds. Warm birds jump from twig to nest to ground. They sing their songs without flaw. Not a cue is missed. The notes carry out over the patches of wheat and flax where they come apart and fall, quick showers on the new fields.

Large bees drift sideways from flower to flower. The bumble-bee has a round body the color of candy, lovely enough to kiss. When I made that mistake my grandfather gave me a heaped bowl of raspberries, with sugar and cream, and while I wept great tears I ate them all.

Older now, I notice that the hours must pass even as do pretty flowers. Left behind is a field with bits of time bending in the wind, each one checked for nectar by a thoughtful bee that will dance a map in the air to remind me where a lost day can be found. Then I will feel a sudden sting for neglecting the search for what is most sweet.

Minnows II

It seems nature has many clocks, all running at once, set to different times. Some are as big as Wyoming, some the size of a nameless creek. If you listened closely, the minnows were black seconds ticking, and it's hard, but I caught one. In the palm of my hand it jumped and tickled and nibbled my skin so I was amused and a bit scared because I was sure that seconds must not be kept from ticking. And anyhow, it had already escaped back into the icy creek. The day was warm and thick as violets. I wondered if I should tell someone that I had been bitten by time and it wasn't so bad.

Prairie Farmstead

On the great empty plains the sky is the main thing, the center of life, it is what is above, all around, you are always trying to keep your balance standing on the very tip of a mountain peak. In sunshine five miles away the dark clump of trees looks an inch wide and a pencil line high. When closer the patch of woods are full of old cottonwoods that surround the farm buildings with a stockade of autumn color. Those that live inside the enclosure are safe for now. The wheat field is plowed. The corn still unpicked but dry, its rustling in the breeze adding more music to the air. Cows are in the pasture with its shallow creek. But when night and cold approach everyone returns with purpose to the farmyard. The farmer with tractor lights on drives in road-speed up the dirt trail into the yard. The lingering cows, now aware of the sudden dark, trot in single file up the deeply cut pasture path to the solid barn. The farmhouse lights have come on and throw warm yellow into the dark. Those still outside with chores they must finish know there is something they cannot name, a chill they feel not from the frost. Then the animals watch the humans closely. When the first call of the owl floats out of the cottonwoods the night has begun. The sentry is in place until morning light. All is well.

A Poet with No Business Sense:
In Praise of Tom Hennen

by Thomas R. Smith

In 1974 a young poet named Tom Hennen, living on the edge
of western Minnesota, published his first collection, a hand-
some, appealingly titled chapbook, *The Heron with No Business
Sense*. A graceful brush-and-ink sketch of a heron embellished
the yellow front cover, with a snapshot on the reverse of the
poet posing a little stiffly against a backdrop of flat, feature-
less prairie and a pine tree, its branches equally accommodat-
ing sun and shadow.

The Heron with No Business Sense belonged to a chapbook
series produced by the Minnesota Writers' Publishing House
(MWPH), a publishing cooperative founded in 1972 and mod-
eled on a successful Swedish prototype. Backed by the consid-
erable prestige of Robert and Carol Bly, MWPH proposed to
strike a blow for midwestern literature against bicoastal dom-
ination, showcasing the work of several distinctive Minne-
sota poets, among them Franklin Brainard, Louis Jenkins, and
Thomas McGrath. Trained as a printer, Tom Hennen operated
MWPH's 1250 Multilith press in the garage of his residence in
Morris, Minnesota. These days you'd pay dearly for almost any
of those seminal MWPH chapbooks on the collectors' market.

With publication of this long-overdue collected poems,
readers at large may now discover one of the Midwest's best
and most underappreciated poets. Taking his prose poem

"What the Plants Say" as a combination *ars poetica* and autobiographical statement, the perceptive reader can divine much of what I want to say about Tom Hennen in this afterword:

> Tree, give up your secret. How can you be so satisfied? Why don't you need to change location, look for a better job, find prettier scenery, or even want to get away from people?
>
> Grass, you don't care where you turn up. You appear running loose in the oat field, out of a crack in a city street. You are the first word in the vocabulary of the earth. How is it that you are able to grow so near the lake without falling in? How can you be so alert for the early frost, bend in the slightest breeze, and yet be so hard to break that you are still there, quiet, green, among the ruins of others?
>
> Weed, it is you with your bad reputation that I love the most. Teach me not to care what anyone has to say about me. Help me to be in the world for no purpose at all except for the joy of sunlight and rain. Keep me close to the edge, where everything wild begins.

I

Tom Hennen was born in Morris, Minnesota, in 1942. Country people of limited financial means, his parents worked a series of rented farms in western Minnesota. When Hennen was nine, his father moved the family to California in pursuit of a change of employment, returning to Minnesota less than a year later. After graduating high school, Hennen served for a short time in the Marine Corps, but before long was back in Morris. In 1965, after an abandoned attempt at college and a footloose young adulthood, Hennen married and went to work as a printer. The printing trade, however, proved ultimately not to Hennen's taste. In the mid-70s he found more fulfilling employment with the state's Department of Natural Resources wildlife section out of the Morris office. In 1992 he continued his outdoor work as a wildlife technician at the Sand Lake National Wildlife Refuge, north of Aberdeen, South Dakota.

Now retired and living in St. Paul, a widower with two children and grandchildren around the Twin Cities, he writes, "When the grandkids are grown, it's the country again."[1] Indeed, for livelihood and inspiration, Tom Hennen has gravitated so consistently toward the Minnesota-South Dakota prairie land as to make it difficult to imagine him a city dweller for long.

Early views of the poet setting out on the path to publication suggest a mild, somewhat diffident personality. Minnesota poet John Calvin Rezmerski, in his introduction to *The Heron with No Business Sense*, alludes to financial and marital difficulties of a kind not foreign to creative introverts and which we might have deduced from Hennen's poems from that period, such as "Looking at the Windmill":

> My kids come back from the long walk
> With their hands full of stones.
> They sense that my foundations
> Are shaky.

---

1. Private communication with the author.

They stay up late
To play with me
And humor me
While all night not talking
I duck in and out of air caves.

I am the distant windmill they know to look at
Moved by the least breeze.

"Tom does everything the hard way," asserts Rezmerski, proceeding to detail some of Hennen's woes.[2] Following so closely on the 60s, during which Bob Dylan's "there's no success like failure, and failure's no success at all" was heard by many as a positive rallying cry, we might suspect an element of bohemian romanticizing here, but the trouble seems serious enough. In fact, difficulty and failure supply a constant, perhaps necessary ground note to Hennen's music, which, though plain, is far from simple.

Hennen's second chapbook, *The Hole in the Landscape Is Real*, an exquisite hand-printed edition from James Gremmels's Prairie Gate Press at the University of Minnesota, Morris, followed in 1976. After that, Hennen published nothing until 1981, when the literary journal *Great River Review*, then based in Winona, Minnesota, featured thirteen new poems in the same spare style as Hennen's previous work. The editor's introduction reveals the usual varied writer's résumé—"busboy, construction laborer, dishwasher, migrant

2. John Calvin Rezmerski, introduction to *The Heron with No Business Sense*, by Tom Hennen (Minnesota Writers' Publishing House, 1974).

worker in the bean fields, and... stage hand for a small theater."[3] To this recitation, Hennen adds intriguingly: "On one trip back to Minnesota... pretty sure I gave Jack Kerouac a ride from Nevada to Wyoming."[4] From the *Great River Review* feature, "I Wish It Were Different" compactly summarizes the strengths and weaknesses of Hennen's position during this period of apparent struggle:

It's only when I'm alone
That the tree
Will let its needles surround
Me shining
Deep in its mental state
Of abnormal
Well being.[5]

If the reader detects in the early Hennen an affinity with the Robert Bly of *Silence in the Snowy Fields*, the resemblance is not coincidental, for Hennen belongs to a generation of Minnesota poets formatively influenced and inspired by Bly. If Bly's poetry put rural Minnesota on the world literary map, there were more than a few young neophytes ready to homestead there. Certainly, many served a period of apprenticeship under the sway of the elder Norwegian-American poet before arriving at their mature styles.

---

3. *Great River Review* 3, no. 2 (1981): 202.

4. Ibid.

5. This poem appears in *Darkness Sticks to Everything* as part of the prose poem "Two Things."

Although Hennen logged a couple of years of college coursework, he has always been something of an outrider of higher education. In addition to scattered studies at Vermilion Community College in Ely and, with Bill Holm and Philip Dacey, at Southwest Minnesota State University in Marshall in the early 1990s, Hennen had "tried a few classes" at the University of Minnesota, Morris, in the early 1960s.[6] Hennen's later forays into college education were generally aimed not at literary studies but at vocational advancement, for purposes of procuring full-time rather than seasonal employment with the DNR.

One far-reaching result of Hennen's college ventures was his discovery of Bly through his teacher and future publisher, James Gremmels. One beautiful day in May 1963, encouraged by Gremmels, Hennen and a friend made the hour's drive to the Bly farm in Madison, dropping in unannounced on the poet and his wife. The two young men were kindly received by the Blys, and even got to talk poetry with James Wright, then staying in Robert's famous remodeled chicken coop. Hennen and his friend left late that day, both "loaded down with books,"[7] and Hennen with increased determination to write his own poems, already well underway.

Hennen recalls tantalizingly one occasion on which Bly and Wright, accompanied by Thomas McGrath and Frederick Manfred, donned suits and ties to read together at the newly

---

6. Private communication with author.
7. Ibid.

opened university at Morris, to celebrate the presence of an institution of higher learning on their edge of the state. Hennen remembers the four writers volunteering their services without pay. Poor attendance of the underpublicized reading didn't noticeably dampen the four friends' spirits. Around this time, according to Hennen, Wright was turned down for a teaching position at Morris. One can only wonder at the difference such a post might have meant to Wright and his career, not to mention to American poetry.

2

Since Hennen has eschewed the writing of autobiographical and critical prose, we must make educated guesses at the extent of his reading. The old Chinese poets, a fondness for which Hennen shares with the 1960s Bly and Wright, must surely figure in the mix. In "Knowing Nothing" Hennen plays a latter-day Tu Fu or Han-shan:

> The hole in the landscape is real.
> I can walk through it and back again.
> Every time I do
> My clothes look baggier.
> My hair sticks out.
> My boots become untied.
> My coat unbuttoned.
> My education gone.
> I don't care anymore how the world thinks.
>
> I only know that the snow
> Has reached my knees.

Like the great Chinese poets, Hennen is a poet of land-scape. In staying close to the earth, both in his life and work, he brings to his poems a specificity of detail beyond the reach of less knowledgeable and attentive observers. And like the Chinese poets, along with Bly and Wright, Hennen is not averse to an occasional title competing in length with the poem itself. My favorite is "If You Bite a Wood Tick in Two with Your Teeth It Can Give You Rocky Mountain Spotted Fever."

In his talent for the poetic image, Hennen recalls another midwestern master of the image, Ted Kooser. Anyone familiar with the Nebraska poet's work will recognize in Hennen a spiritual blood brother. Both poets share an ability to move a brief poem directly to its central image with extreme economy of expression. "Summer Night Air" is a perfect example:

Night doesn't fall
It rises
Out of low spots
Tree trunks
And the back
Of the old cow
I'm bringing home to milk.

Even more condensed is the aphoristic "Cold in the Trees":

The hoot
Of the owl
Is large enough
To carry off a whole sheep.

Hennen knows how to freight even a four-line poem with appeals to multiple senses. Though his visual strengths are ample, I am struck particularly by his use of the sense of smell to evoke complex and delicate emotions. In "Smelling a Stone in the Middle of Winter," the stone "smells as though / It's been wrapped in flowers / As your dress does / On a spring afternoon." In "Finding Horse Skulls on a Day That Smelled of Flowers," new grass makes "the scent of the earth visible."

In Hennen we notice what the Jungians would call intuitive and sensate qualities coexisting at high levels. Again, we can compare Hennen with Robert Bly, though Bly balances more to the intuitive side and Hennen more to the sensate. Hennen came of age at a time when the so-called deep image waxed strong on the American literary scene, a movement well fitted to Hennen's drift toward inwardness and introversion. To the extent that his poems value and celebrate solitude, the earth, elemental presences, and the inner life, Hennen remains one of the purest inheritors of the deep image.

Bly's influence on Hennen also extends to the many world poets Bly has translated and with whom Hennen is certainly familiar. Coming to mind are the Scandinavian modernists, who also have adored the old poets of China and Japan, including Olav H. Hauge, Rolf Jacobsen, Tomas Tranströmer, and perhaps especially Harry Martinson, whose poems share with Hennen's a ground-level view of the northern earth in its seasonal moods and displays.

Although Hennen writes accurately and vividly of all the seasons on the Minnesota-Dakota prairie, his heart belongs more to the transitional seasons than to summer or winter. His is a landscape of long, oppressive winters in which dreams of thaw become intermingled with a yearning for personal regeneration. Milder weather seems to suit Hennen's moderate temperament best. Those who have lived in the far north know that the longing for springtime can itself be a torment during the extended darkness and cold of winter. The piercing desire that permeates Hennen's poems is at its most elemental level a desire to distance oneself from death, as in these elegant, sensorily evocative lines in "Finding Horse Skulls on a Day That Smelled of Flowers":

> Where the sun touched shining bone
> It was warm
> As though the horses were dreaming
> In the spring afternoon
> With night
> Still miles away.

In 1983, two more Hennen books appeared, *Looking into the Weather* and *Selected Poems 1963–1983*.[8] This small feast was followed by another decade of famine, broken finally by the appearance in 1993 of *Love for Other Things: New and Selected Poems*.[9] Robert Bly, in his introduction, "Returning Some Sort

---

8. *Looking into the Weather* (Minneota, MN: Westerheim Press, 1983). *Selected Poems 1963–1983* (Morris, MN: Prairie Gate Press, 1983).

9. *Love for Other Things: New and Selected Poems* (Moorhead, MN: Dacotah Territory, 1993).

of Thanks," justly paid tribute to Hennen's "strange ability to bring immense amounts of space, often uninhabited space, into his mind and so into the whole poem."

3

Four more years passed until the publication of *Crawling Out the Window*, a collection of prose poems from Black Hat Press (Goodhue, Minnesota), in 1997. *Crawling Out the Window* appeared to mark a startling change of direction for Hennen, though in fact several of the poems dated back at least a decade.

Still Hennen was no stranger to the prose poem form; no poet in Minnesota could be, with two of the prose poem's contemporary American masters, Bly and Louis Jenkins, prominent on the regional literary scene. Hennen also cites as inspiration Francis Ponge's "object" prose poems, which he first encountered in Cid Corman's translations and admired for what he calls their "technical" quality.[10] Where Hennen's previous poems exemplified a laconic, even reserved diction, the prose poem gave Hennen permission to stretch out, say more than he'd been either able or willing to before, and register a richness of detail his more pared-down verse poems couldn't comfortably accommodate. Louis Jenkins has called the prose poem "a formal poem with unspecified limits."[11] In *Crawling*

---

10. Private communication with author.
11. Louis Jenkins, *Nice Fish* (Duluth: Holy Cow! Press, 1995).

Out the Window, Hennen found room to move freely within the rectangular tract of the paragraph, which in his practice contains, to echo Bly, "immense amounts of space."

In the title poem of that collection, Hennen posits two kinds of people: one for whom life comes easily "like warm rain," and another for whom life is more problematic. The first metaphorically "falls south" in what could be called the Great Divide of things. On the other hand, Hennen's old totem, the heron with no business sense, haunts the hapless dreamer who "falls north," as the poet himself has clearly done. If you are such a person, says Hennen, "You watch the geese and are sure you can fly."

Given Hennen's love of the outdoors, his repeated references to wild geese and other migrant waterfowl shouldn't surprise us. If it seems banal and obvious to invoke the freedom these winged creatures suggest, we could complicate matters by adding that Hennen's other totem seems to be the ephemeral yet persistent insect life of the prairie. Hennen writes with as much sympathy for insects as did the classical Japanese haiku poet Issa. Perhaps the geese embody a high-flying potential Hennen feels in himself, and the insects a homelier cleaving to earth. In "In the Sky of Winter," he brings a tenderly personal empathy to the frozen fliers he discovers "in the tiny cases of their bodies, alive, some of them, but still as fallen twigs or stones."

Hennen's prose poems testify eloquently to a hard-won comfort level with the poet's own particular gifts and limitations. He is secure in his voice, which he'll now allow to become relaxed, even conversational and comic if he chooses. If the early poems give glimpses of one in retreat from a world ruled by "an outgoing personality and a knack for business," as he puts it in "Crawling Out the Window," the later work reveals a man firm in his chosen place, among the elemental presences of nature, all of which, he says in "Looking for the Differences," have their own souls. "I watch where I step and see that the fallen leaf, old broken glass, an icy stone are placed in exactly the right spot on the earth, carefully, royalty in their own country."

Crawling Out the Window is one of the greatest prose poem collections written by an American. It can stand confidently and unapologetically in the company of Bly's *The Morning Glory* and Jenkins's *An Almost Human Gesture*, the happy marriage of a content and its ideal form. Hennen continues to develop the prose poem in the new poems in *Darkness Sticks to Everything*, several of which can stand with his best, including "What the Bees Found," "Corn Picking 1956 — Afternoon Break," "Plains Spadefoot Toad," and "Outdoor Photos." The last, especially, exemplifies a gentle humor that has increasingly become a hallmark of Hennen's later work. One can extrapolate from these sentences a policy of intimacy and tact toward the reader, not to mention an approach to life, that is almost courtly: "Still, even if we are only on display for a moment in a water drop as it clings to a pine needle, it is expected that we be on our best behavior, hair combed, jacket buttoned, no vulgar language. Smiling is not necessary, but a pleasant attitude is helpful, and would be, I think, appreciated."

As a whole, the new poems in this volume are a generous and welcome addition to the Hennen opus. Whether looking back, as some do, toward Hennen's boyhood on the farm, as in the gorgeous "Outside Hay Pile 1956," or, as many others do, toward the lasting assurances of earth, each is founded on an understated, powerful affirmation of the goodness of work, life, family, and the kinship of creatures. There are also a couple of love poems, their emotional directness even more disarming in view of this reserved poet's earlier reticence:

> Then the sky appeared in blue patches
> Among slow clouds,
> Oak leaves came out on the trees,
> Grass suddenly became green,
> Filled with small animals that sing.
> All the parts of spring were gathering.
> The earth was being created all over again
> One piece at a time
> Just for you.

("Found on the Earth")

4

Revisiting Tom Hennen's poems for this essay, I'm struck once more by their essential timelessness. While it's true that some of the earlier poems lose themselves in the elemental archetypes of the more derivative deep image practitioners, Hennen quickly finds his own road, upon which he is occasionally accompanied not only by Robert Bly and James Wright but by Harry Martinson and, indeed (and why not?), Jack Kerouac too. Hennen's mature tone is level, almost Taoist, with a tempered knowledge of self and world. Hennen avoids poetic fashion and speaks without pretension, though not unmusically, of an ancient way of being on and with the earth, which even in our time of increasingly catastrophic climate change somehow manages to persist. His work is in basic sympathy with the native poets the ethnographer Frances Densmore recorded almost a century ago among the prairie and woodland tribes of the upper Midwest where Hennen was born.

Such a stance does not impress the urban poetry tastemakers always running with the newest, most attention-getting verbal displays. To that world, what Tom Hennen does may indeed look a lot like failure. But Hennen has clearly made his peace with those perceptions long ago. His southwestern Minnesota neighbor, teacher, and friend, the late Bill Holm, argued in his essay "The Music of Failure" that "The heart can be filled anywhere on earth."[12] Americans have tended to judge unkindly those who, chosen by a place, return the favor, forsaking other "higher" ambitions that might call them elsewhere. Despite the ordinary defeats of life, Hennen has kept faith with his poems, celebrating and illuminating his native place.

I have admired Tom Hennen's work for many years, and I rejoice in the publication of *Darkness Sticks to Everything*, a

---

12. Bill Holm, "The Music of Failure: Variations on an Idea" in *The Heart Can Be Filled Anywhere on Earth: Minneota, Minnesota* (Minneapolis: Milkweed Editions, 1996), 60.

jubilant event in American poetry. Hennen is one of those poets we return to when we long to relearn what attracted us to poetry in the first place. Again and again, his poems pull us back from pretension to honesty, away from things, as Lawrence or Whitman might say, not of the soul. Time after time, he calls us closer to earth, though not at the cost of clipping our wings. He has written poetry for all the right reasons and ranks with the true and truthful ones, whom we can trust implicitly, and who, to borrow his words a last time, "will be talked about for years to come around a fireplace on sparkling cold nights when the winter is so long and the darkness so deep that the heart of the earth might break."

Index of Titles

Index of First Lines

About the Author

Tom Hennen was born in Morris, Minnesota, and grew up in a farming family. His poetry is informed by a lifelong and intimate relationship with the prairie and a professional life that kept him working outdoors—first with the Minnesota Department of Natural Resources and then as a wildlife technician at the Sand Lake National Wildlife Refuge. "In winter I'd get laid off," he says. "It was bad for retirement, but good for writing."

Hennen is the author of six books of poetry and the recipient of the Bachelor Farmer Lifetime Achievement in the Arts. His poems have appeared in several anthologies, including Garrison Keillor's *Good Poems;* a volume of selected poems is being translated into Norwegian. He lives in Minnesota.

JIM HARRISON is a poet, novelist, and screenwriter. He is the author of *Legends of the Fall, Dalva,* and *The Shape of the Journey: New and Collected Poems* (Copper Canyon Press).

THOMAS R. SMITH is a poet, teacher and editor. His recent books of poems include *Waking Before Dawn* and *The Foot of the Rainbow* (Red Dragonfly Press).

Poetry is vital to language and living. Since 1972, Copper Canyon Press has published extraordinary poetry from around the world to engage the imaginations and intellects of readers, writers, booksellers, librarians, teachers, students, and donors.

WE ARE GRATEFUL FOR THE MAJOR SUPPORT PROVIDED BY:

THE PAUL G. ALLEN
FAMILY FOUNDATION

THE MAURER FAMILY
FOUNDATION

NATIONAL
ENDOWMENT
FOR THE ARTS

WASHINGTON STATE
ARTS COMMISSION

Anonymous

Arcadia Fund

John Branch

Diana and Jay Broze

Beroz Ferrell & The Point, LLC

Mimi Gardner Gates

Gull Industries, Inc.
on behalf of William and Ruth True

Mark Hamilton and Suzie Rapp

Carolyn and Robert Hedin

Steven Myron Holl

Rhoady and Jeanne Marie Lee

Maureen Lee and Mark Busto

New Mexico Community Foundation

H. Stewart Parker

Penny and Jerry Peabody

Joseph C. Roberts

Cynthia Lovelace Sears and Frank Buxton

The Seattle Foundation

Charles and Barbara Wright

The dedicated interns and faithful
volunteers of Copper Canyon Press

To learn more about underwriting Copper Canyon Press titles,
please call 360-385-4925 ext. 103

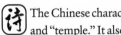 The Chinese character for poetry is made up of two parts: "word" and "temple." It also serves as pressmark for Copper Canyon Press.

This book is set in MVB Verdigris, a text face by Mark van Bronkhorst, with display type set in Monotype Garamond. Book design by VJBScribe. Printed on archival-quality stock at McNaughton & Gunn, Inc.